Count On It!

Two

Dana Meachen Rau

Marshall Cavendish
Benchmark
New York

Two boys.

Two legs.

Two eyes.

Two eggs.

Two shoes.

Two sleds.

Two wheels.

Two beds.

Two!

19

Words We Know

beds

boys

eggs

eyes

20

legs

shoes

sleds

wheels

Index

Page numbers in **boldface** are illustrations.

About the Author

Dana Meachen Rau is the author of many other titles in the Bookworms series, as well as other nonfiction and early reader books. She lives in Burlington, Connecticut, with her husband and two children.

With thanks to the Reading Consultants:

Nanci Vargus, Ed.D., is an Assistant Professor of Elementary Education at the University of Indianapolis.

Beth Walker Gambro is an Adjunct Professor at the University of St. Francis in Joliet, Illinois.

Marshall Cavendish Benchmark
99 White Plains Road
Tarrytown, New York 10591-5502
www.marshallcavendish.us

Library of Congress Cataloging-in-Publication Data

Rau, Dana Meachen, 1971–
Two / by Dana Meachen Rau.
p. cm. — (Bookworms. Count on it!)
Summary: "Identifies things that inherently come in twos and lists other examples"—Provided by publisher.
Includes index.
ISBN 978-0-7614-2967-8
1. Two (The number)—Juvenile literature. 2. Number concept—Juvenile literature. I. Title. II. Series.
QA141.3.R283 2009
513—dc22
2007024618

Editor: Christina Gardeski
Publisher: Michelle Bisson
Designer: Virginia Pope
Art Director: Anahid Hamparian

Photo Research by Anne Burns Images

The photographs in this book are used with permission and through the courtesy of:
SuperStock: pp. 1, 11, 21TR BananaStock; pp. 7, 15, 19, 20BR, 21BR age fotostock; pp. 13, 21BL SuperStock.
Jupiter Images: pp. 3, 20TR Noble Stock; pp. 5, 21TL Marcie Jan Bronstein; pp. 9, 20BL Push. *Jay Mallin*: pp. 17, 20TL.

Printed in Malaysia
1 3 5 6 4 2